Weddings around the World

Written by Margaret MacDonald

Picture Dictionary

bride and groom

cake

ceremony

Read the picture dictionary. You will find these words in the book.

clothes

food

guests

When people get married,
they have a ceremony.
The ceremony
is called a wedding.

garland
fire

The man getting married is called the groom. The woman getting married is called the bride.

veil
bouquet

The bride and the groom
wear special clothes
for their wedding.
Some brides wear
a very special dress.

headdress
jacket

Guests go to a wedding.
They go to the ceremony.
They bring gifts
for the bride and groom.

ribbon
box

There is special food
at a wedding.
The bride and groom
and the guests
eat the special food.

nuts
fruit

Some brides and grooms have a big wedding cake.
They cut the cake.
The guests eat the cake.

frosting
layers

Activity Page

1. Draw a three-layer wedding cake.
   Each layer will be a different size.
   The bottom layer is the largest.
   The top layer is the smallest.

2. Draw a bride and groom
   cutting the cake.
   Then write a caption.

Do you know the dictionary words?